I'M FINE!

Copyright © 2004 by Mandana Hoveyda

All rights reserved. No part of this book may be reproduced in any form without written permission from the publisher.

Library of Congress Cataloging in Publication Number: 2003095939

ISBN: 1-931686-66-1

Printed in China

Typeset in Brillo, Obsolete, Litterbox

Illustrations by mandana hoveyda

Design by bryn ashburn

Collage by bryn ashburn, karen onorato, and cheyenne mcgarvey

Distributed in North America
by Chronicle Books
85 Second Street
San Francisco, CA 94105

10  9  8  7  6  5  4  3  2  1

Quirk Books
215 Church Street
Philadelphia, PA 19106
www.quirkbooks.com

# I'm Fine!

## A Really Helpful Guide to the First 100 Days After Your Breakup

by Mandana Hoveyda

QUIRK BOOKS
PHILADELPHIA

for Mojagan Jaypour

(Special thanks to Mom,
Dad, and Roxy.)

# INTRODUCTION

Some people say that every day love teaches them more than anything they've ever learned in school. I would agree.

Especially the part where he broke up with me.

It was March, it was cold, and it was raining. We were at a bar. I had just ordered a beer.

I was left with two pints and no plans. Well, except to drink two pints.

On my way out later that night I overheard someone say that it was in this very bar that Dylan Thomas drank himself to death.

After that, a whole new world opened up to me.

A world where I felt a wide range of conflicting emotions every single minute. (Anger, hostility, and revenge were just a few of them.) A world where solace could be found in yoga, religion, food, exercise, dieting, liquor, holistic medicine, facials, manicures, pedicures, animals, magazines, books, TV, psychics, and Barneys. A world where it was entirely possible to lose fifteen pounds in one week and then gain seventeen in another.

<6>

But most of all I learned that I was not alone. Everyone has gone through breakups. It sucks. And of course it's only natural that you might all of a sudden have very dark thoughts, like what if your boyfriend were suddenly found at the bottom of the reservoir with his leg tied to a rock?

To keep those thoughts out of your mind, and your body off the couch, here is a guide to help you navigate each and every of the first 100 days after your breakup. After all, you've spent every day for the past eight months sharing your waffles with your significant other—you may be at a loss for what to do on that first day when it's just you.

And remember, if I could make it through my breakup, anyone can.

Good luck!

## ☑ Day 1:

- Get up.
- Go to work.
- And cry.

Don't look at the cute old e-mails he sent you. Don't sit and stare at the phone. Take all of his pictures off your desk. And don't call him. Call your best friend and ask her to sleep over. You'll understand tomorrow morning.

<8>

<9>

# Day 2:

Waking up alone is **no** fun.
Good thing your best friend
   slept over. Now you can cry
   to her when you wake up. As an
added bonus she kept you

   from calling him last night.
Now get out of your house. And
unplug your answering
   machine. You don't want to be
hoping that you'll get a call

   from him while you were out.

<10>

YOU HAVE NO NEW MESSAGES.

YOU HAVE NO NEW MESSAGES.

YOU HAVE NO NEW MESSAGES.

YOU HAVE NO NEW MESSAGES.

YOU HAVE NO NEW MESSAGES.

# Day 3:

Don't call him. Don't e-mail him. It's OK to think about him, but he doesn't have to know that.

<12>

<13>

## ☑ Day 4:

Call a therapist. This may sound cliché, but in two weeks when your friends start to get sick of listening to you bitch about the breakup, and you feel crazy because it still hurts, you'll thank me.

<15>

# 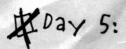Day 5:

Print out all the old e-mails
he sent you. Don't read them.
Put them in an envelope
with all your pictures of him
(except the two worst, save
those) and mementos of the
two of you and send them to
your mother. Tell her to
put them in the basement,
someplace where you won't
stumble across them until
you're ready.

# ☑Day 6:

It's been almost a week: Time to white out his name, address, and number from your phone book. Write someone else's name in that space so when you get desperate and really really want to call him you can't. And trust me, you can't scratch Wite-Out off. I've tried.

<18>

# Day 7

Time to get his clothes out of your apartment. Yes, you can deal with this. Yes, even the white T-shirt you've been sleeping in. I know it looks great on you but these are drastic times. Now, get a big garbage bag, throw everything in, and toss it in the trash. Outside.

And cry.

It's therapeutic.

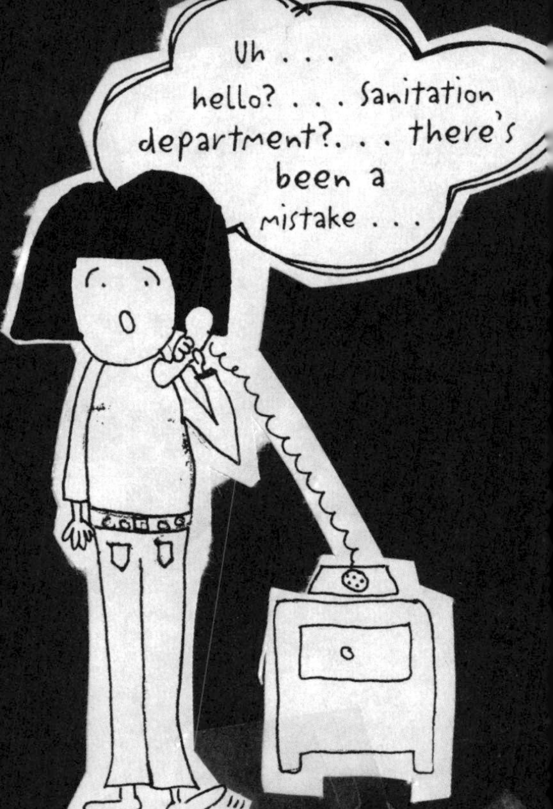
Uh . . .
hello? . . . Sanitation department?. . . there's been a mistake . . .

# Day 8:

Go away. If at all possible visit your parents. You can sit in front of the TV and someone will bring you cookies. You can cry and have someone hug you and hand you hankies. You can be pathetic. And if your parents are anything like mine, they will start to drive you so crazy going on and on about their taxes that you will start to feel something other than completely despondent. You'll feel annoyed. Congratulations, you're moving on.

<22>

<23>

OH JOHN . . . .

OH SUZI,
I LOVE YOU
DON'T EVER
LEAVE ME . . . .

<24>

<25>

## DAY 9:
Watch mindless TV. You're not ready for any heavy plot lines, seeing as the only thing you're thinking about is your ex.

# Day 10:

Don't ask friends what he is
up to. OK, if you have to,
ask a friend who you're sure
will not say a word to him.
Just don't let it get back
to him.

<26>

<27>

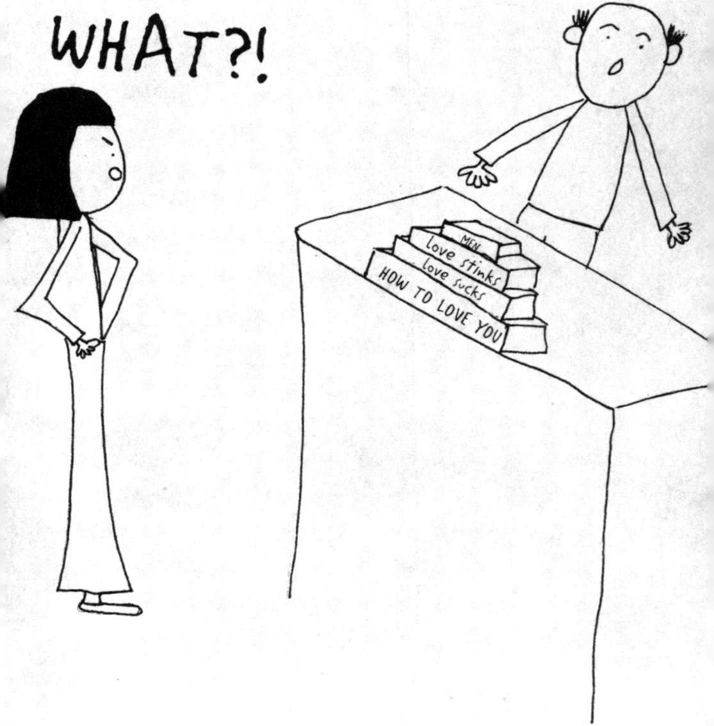
WHAT?!
MEN
love stinks
love sucks
HOW TO LOVE YOU

# Day 11:

Time to turn to a higher order:

Self-help books.

<29>

# Day 12:

Stop listening to lyrics of songs. Especially love songs. Or songs about breaking up. Whatever you do, don't make this a time to expand your musical horizons and listen to country music, unless, as a friend of mine says, you can either laugh at it or find the beauty in the human experience of lost love.

OK, not a lot of us can do that. Try techno—there are no lyrics.

I NEVER FOUND LOVE AGAIN AND NEVER EVER RECOVERED . . .

<31>

<32>

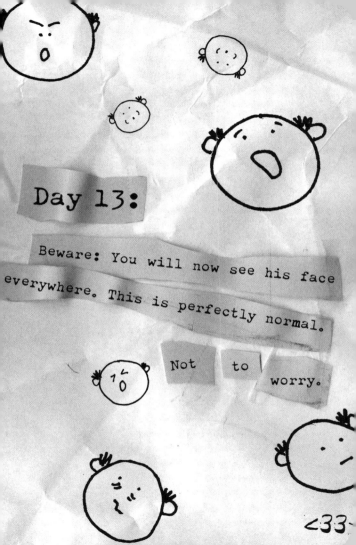

# Day 14

Don't even bother opening the paper. You're not ready, trust me. The only thing that will jump out at you will be the sports page.

<34>

# Day 15

Do not drive by his house to see if the lights are on. Do not drive by his house to see if there are any "strange cars" out front. And if you're thinking about going through his garbage, that's just gross.

<36>

<37>

☑ **Day 16:**

- Go out to dinner with friends. NO COUPLES!!!
- Have a drink and talk about him.
- At this point you probably won't cry. Probably.

<38>

WAAA . . .
My life is over . . .
Please earth open now and swallow me whole . . .
WAAA . . .
HELP ME GOD
Oh Satan, take John as your own!!!

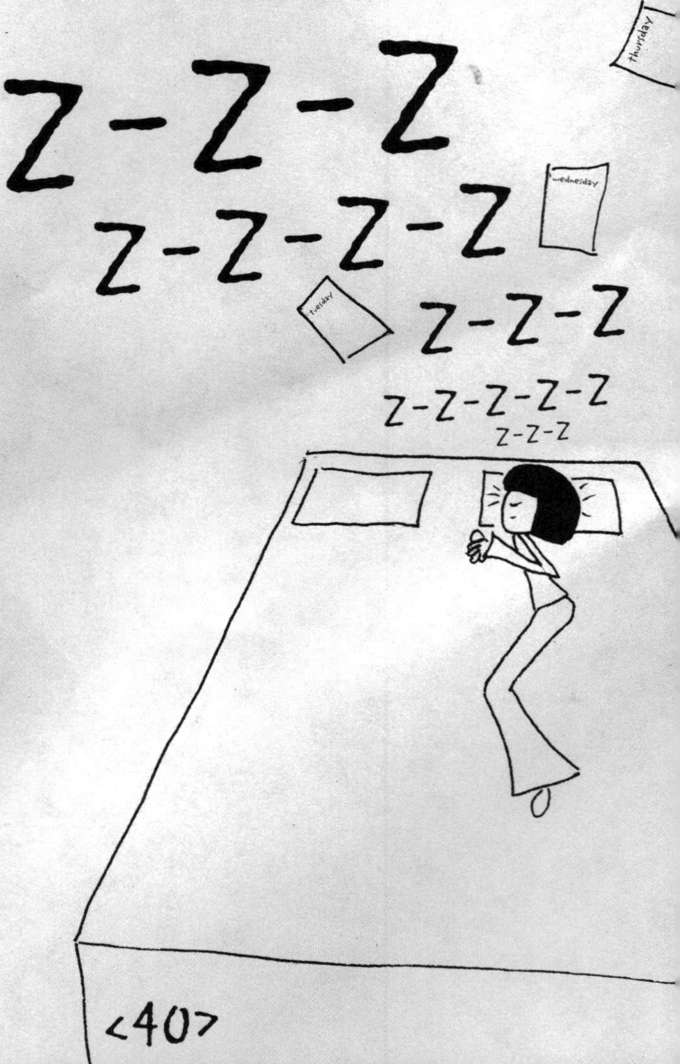
thursday
Z-Z-Z
wednesday
Z-Z-Z-Z
tuesday
Z-Z-Z
Z-Z-Z-Z-Z
Z-Z-Z

# Day 17:

So, you can't sleep. That's to be expected.
But sleeping pills leave

you **groggy**

and drinking leaves you

**boozy**. I like

melatonin. It works

like a charm.

friday

saturday

sunday

monday

tuesday

wednesday

<41>

# Day 18:

Find a new hobby.
One that will make you
concentrate so that even while you
are watching TV or listening to
music, your mind won't
wander to him.

I like needlepoint.

<42>

<43>

# Day 19

OK, now you can catch up to the rest of the world. It's safe to open the paper. But **don't even go NEAR** the sports page.

44>

<45>

# ~~#~~ Day 20

Go shopping. There is nothing more
comforting than an outrageous hot
pink dress that you'll never wear
but that makes you look smashing.

<46>

<47>

# ~~#~~ Day 21:

- Get a manicure.
- Look more girlie than ever.

<48>

<49>

# Day 22

Get a pedicure. If you ever
it's now. Yes, even if it's

. . . I'll have
them all
airbrushed
please.

<50>

need to have beautiful feet,

the dead of winter and no

one's going to see them.

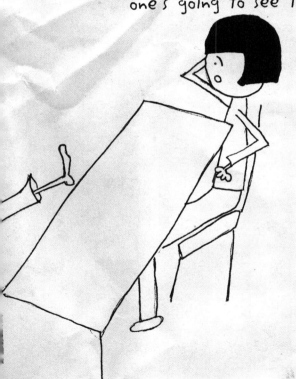

<51>

# Day 23

Go shopping. This time it's shoes.

Get a pair that are open-toed, incredibly high, and impossible to walk in. Remember, at times like these, money is no object.

Even credit card companies understand that.

<52>

<53>

# Day 24:

Time for some dancing. Get a group together and go some place really cheesy. Pretend it's spring break and order Tequila Sunrises.

<54>

<55>

# ~~D~~ Day 25:

Go shopping. Again, money is no
object at a time like this. Buy
clothes that are completely out of
your budget. Getting depressed
about spending too much money is
much easier to deal with than
getting depressed about what's-
his-name.

# DAY 26:

Go to a museum. Museums make you feel incredibly smart and cultured. Which leads to feeling smarter and more cultured than your ex. As a matter of fact, you're on your way to becoming too smart for him!

Oh! NOW I get it.

Now you absolutely CAN'T get back together with him. THAT would be slumming.

<58>

black

<59

☐ DAY 27: Don't call him.

<60>

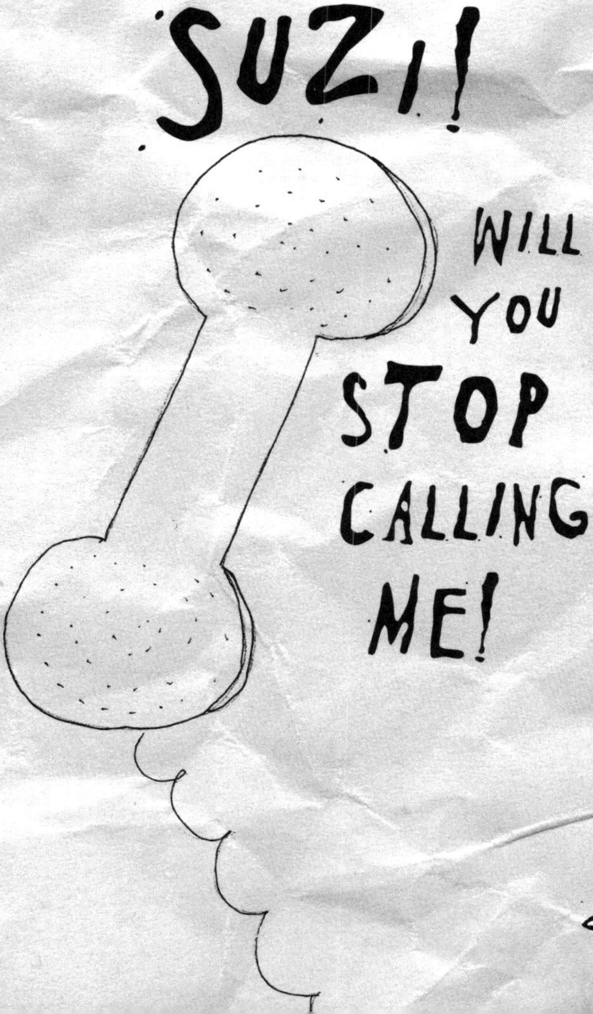
SUZI!
WILL YOU STOP CALLING ME!

In this book
the protagonist is
just like me,
unjustifiably
DUMPED
by a
LOSER!

# Day 28:

Join a book club. OK, no—book clubs are not for spinsters and old maids. They put you right smack dab in the middle of the intellectual loop. And just think how nice it will be to discuss something other than The Big Book of Beer.
_____

# Day 29

Call a psychic. It's good to dabble in the intellectual, but sometimes a girl just needs someone to tell her she's better off without her ex and that her career is about to take off.

<64>

☑ Day 30

Remember to associate EVERYTHING
with him, e.g.:

- I can't go there, we used to go
  to that restaurant.

- We used to take cabs together—
  so I'll walk instead.

- We walked on that street once.
  I'll walk on the next street
  over . . .

<66>

I'd love to,
but I can't . . .
I used to leave the house
with John . . .
MS. HAVISHAM

## Day 31

Rent a documentary. This is the Blockbuster equivalent of an art history class. You will suddenly appear to be one of those smart, artsy chicks. And it's a lot easier than watching two hours of Baroque and Rococo slides.

<68>

. . . mais ze production quality was horrible, as was ze manipulation of ze 1/2 frames.

<69>

Time to go shopping again.

By this point you're feeling bitter . . .

I mean better. And you might run into him. So you've got two choices.

run into him looking like crap,

or run into him looking like someone who would never go out with him.

I tend to lean toward the latter,

but that's just me.

OK, I've worn this tank top for 30 days in a row . . .

When am I going to run into him?

<71>

## Day 33

Remember you can still be anything you want to be. But what? I like to point people toward a great source of inspiration: The Yellow Pages.

Choose something unique. I became a fencer, like with a sword and a mask. Not only did I now have a totally unique new persona, but holding, aiming, and thrusting a sword toward somebody's heart was incredibly fulfilling.

<73>

# Day 34:

You may be feeling like you're getting
to call him (you're not), just to see how
need to hear him say that), just to let

assume this if you don't call him), just to
not), that you can be friends (you can't

Hello, Mr. John?
This is your bank . . .
You're out
of money.

<74>

tronger (you are), strong enough

e's doing (he's doing fine, you don't

im know that you're doing fine (he'll

rove that you're over him (you're

r friendly (forget it), or on speaking

terms (I said forget it!!!).

SUZI! STOP CALLING ME!

<75>

# Day 35:

Call a mutual friend and let her know how well you are doing. It'll get back to him, not to worry.

<76>

Remember those ugly pictures I
told you to save? Get them out.
Show them to some people who
don't know him and ask what
they think.

<78>

<79>

# Day 37:

Think of all the repulsive parts of
his body you didn't like at first
and then started to think were
cute but are really repulsive.

E.g. moles, love handles, weird
teeth, and skin problems.

<81>

# Day 38

**DO NOT** call his house and hang up. Unfortunately, sometimes technology is **NOT** a girl's best friend.

<82>

<83>

<84>

## Day 39:

Read the paper back to front. Then read <u>The Economist</u> and any other in-depth magazines so you know the stories inside and out. It's that smarter thing again.

<85>

☑ Day 40

Think about him farting.

<87>

# Day 41:

Sign up for an acting class. You're going to run into him sooner or later, so you'd better learn how to act indifferent.

<89>

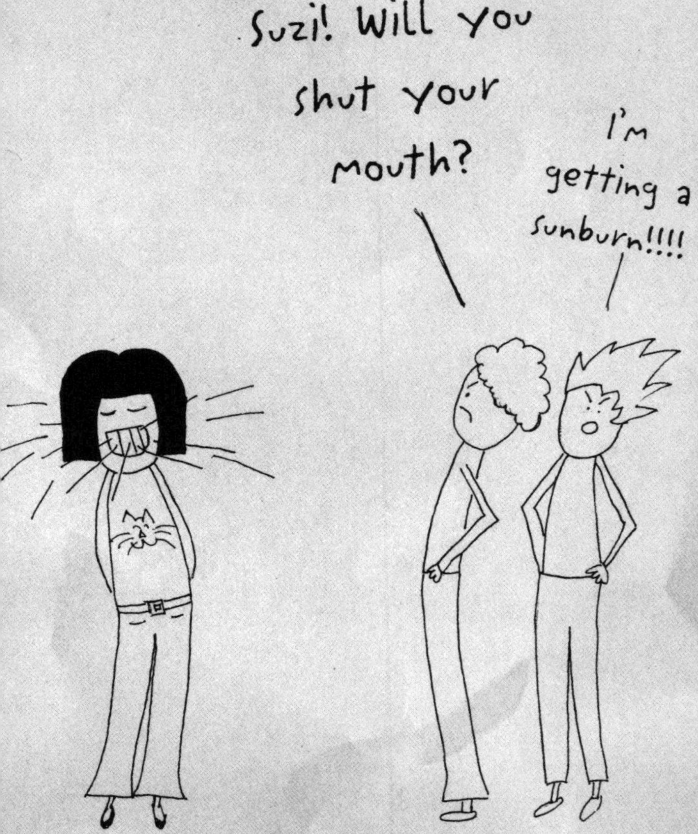
Suzi! Will you shut your mouth?
I'm getting a sunburn!!!!

# Day 42:

Get your teeth cleaned.
Super cleaned.

<91>

# Day 43

Think about how he would call you "Hon" and "Babe" and how you really

hated it.

Yes, you did, even if it was just

at first.

3 MONTHS AGO →

<92>

# Day 44

Throw away all the uncomfortable

underwear you bought when you

were with him.

<94>

<95>

# Day 45:

Color your hair. A distinctive
shade of red always works for
me.

<96>

Everything I hate
about John
_____

1.

# Day 46:

Write a list of all the things you hated about him. Keep it handy so you can look at it every time you think about calling him.

# Day 47

Write a little screenplay starring you. Here's
how it starts: You are walking down th
street, feeling and looking great.

You turn the corner. Cut to a couple walking
toward you. They look very much in love

Cut to a close-up of the girl. She is tall
and blond and very skinny. She looks like a
model. You realize it's your ex with his new
chick. There is no avoiding them.

OK, now it's your turn. Where does it go from here?

Remember what you want to
happen next in this
drama, because it will happen sooner or later.
But you'll be prepared, and you will
pull it off.

Now who says acting lessons don't
come in handy?

<100>

<101>

# ☑ Day 48:

- Write him a mean, nasty letter—i.e. hate mail.
- Then tear it up.
- Never, ever send it, because as my friend Whitney would say, you don't want anything you say in your current state to be permanent and in someone else's possession.

<102>

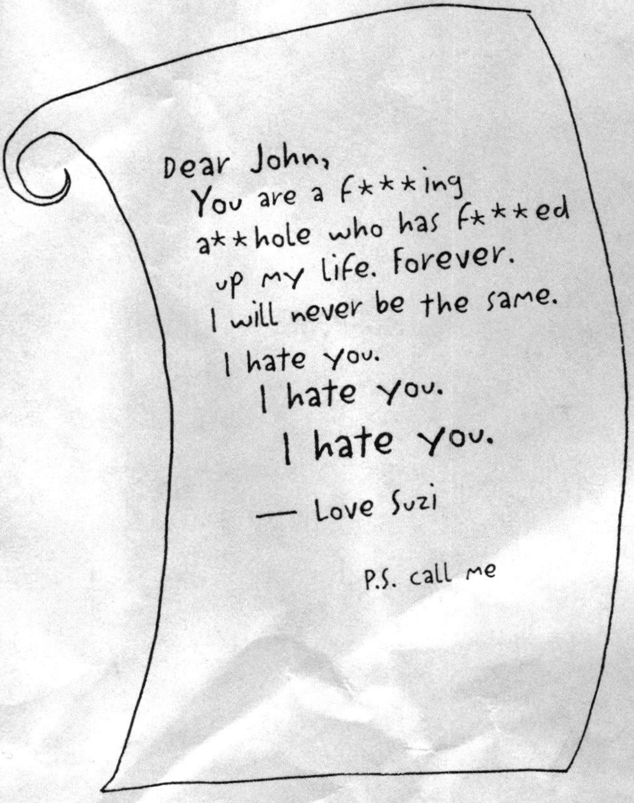
Dear John,
You are a f***ing
a**hole who has f***ed
up my life. Forever.
I will never be the same.
I hate you.
I hate you.
I hate you.
— Love Suzi
P.S. call me

# DAY 49:

Call a girlfriend you haven't seen in forever. Go out. Get drunk. And fill her in on the whole sordid affair.

<105>

Day 50:

LIQUOR

MORE LIQUOR

<106>

# You're halfway there.

Celebrate by getting the most expensive take-out around. Invite a bunch of friends over and get liquored up.

She's gonna vomit again, isn't she?

Get over it Suzi. We're outta here.

<107>

# Day 51

Go to yoga. Twisting yourself
into a pretzel works wonders
for your mind. As an added
bonus, you'll make lots of new
friends.

<109>

# Day 52

Get an herbal wrap
and a mud bath.

<111>

# Day 53

Smoke cigarettes and
drink herbal tea.

# Day 54:

Give thanks to Gloria Steinem, who made it possible for a woman to survive and be happy on her own.

<114>

<115>

Day 55

Remember, artificial insemination

really is an option.

# Day 56

Think about his hair. Like if he
had any on his back or coming
out of his ears or if he had one
really long eyebrow.

<118>

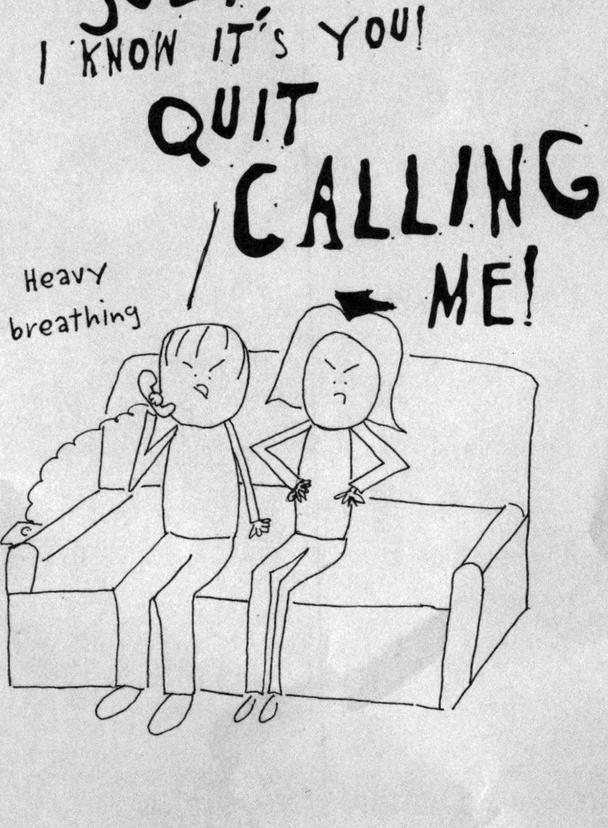
SUZI
I KNOW IT'S YOU!
QUIT CALLING ME!
Heavy breathing

☐ Day 57:

Don't call him.

<121>

# Day 58

Take a spontaneous weekend trip.

Visit old college buddies. Play drinking

games. I can't tell you how much

satisfaction you can get from rolling

a quarter off your nose.

<122>

# ☑ Day 59:

- Barneys. Barneys. Barneys.

- Tell the salesperson that you just broke up with your boyfriend. Let him take it from there.

- If there is no Barneys in your town, move to New York.

<124>

# Day 60:

Take a bubble bath. DO NOT under any circumstances, however, make this the time in your life where you attempt to hold your breath underwater for an inordinate amount of time.

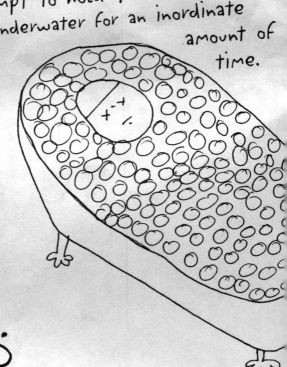

<126>

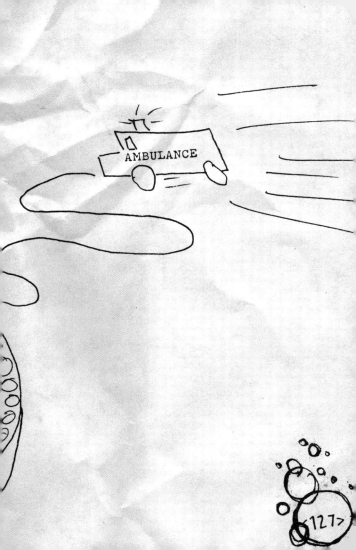

<127>

# Day 61:

Don't call his home answering machine when he's at work just to hear his voice.

BRRRRING

BRRRRING

<128>

AREN'T YOU GONNA ANSWER THAT?
NO. THAT'S JUST MY PSYCHO EX-GIRLFRIEND SUZI ... WANNA PLAY NINTENDO?

# Day 62

My friend Scott and I like to fantasize about our perfect love. It's all very hush-hush. We like to imagine that our new boyfriends will meet us at the JFK airport bar and we all promptly jet off to Paris for a weekend of croissants and amour. That is, after we finish our Cosmopolitans. Make up your own fantasy. It's lots of fun.

<130>

Get a facial. There's nothing I like more than clear skin. Well, maybe good gossip.

<132>

My new boyfriend
JOHN loves my
clear skin . . .

<133>

# ~~#~~ Day 64

Buy a pair of
leather pants.

<134>

I look like a stupid idiot.

# Day 65

Go to the gym. I've heard that some people work out like crazy after a breakup. Not me. I like to sit around and wallow until people stop talking about how bad they feel for me and start talking about how I've gained so much weight.

<136>

<137>

# Day 66:

Throw a party. Preparing and cleaning up will keep your mind very occupied.

<138>

<139>

# Day 67:

- Look for the humor in life.

- Make fun of your ex.

Ha ha ha ha ha

<140>

# DAY 68:

Don't call your parents. They'll only any dates. Then they'll tell you some believable because it's a lie) story daughter met her husband

. . . but you've never even been to the Ukraine . . . how do you know they're not cute?!

Tell her there are 5,000 eligible men waiting for her.

<142>

ask you if you've been out on

unbelievable (as in not
about how their neighbor's

on the Internet.
    Parents have no heart.

<143>

# Day 69:

Expand your vocabulary. Go through the dictionary and pick out a few words. (I like diabolical, disingenuous, and disreputable.) To make sure they stick in your head, use them in a sentence. E.g.: John's behavior after our breakup led me to believe that he is diabolical, disingenuous, and disreputable.

<144>

We broke up 'cause he was diabolical, disingenuous, and disreputable.

Hmmm??? I thought he was cute, cuddly, and congenial???

You need to get your stuff back. I found that telling him that you'll be over to get your stuff works really well. Expect a messenger toting your belongings on your doorstep before you know it.

<146>

<147>

# Day 71:

Change the message on your answering machine and voice mail. You are cheerful. You do not miss him at all. As a matter of fact, you're happier than you've ever been in your life. Leaving people to ask, "Why weren't you this happy when you were going out with him?" Ummmm, good question.

<148>

HEY SUZI,
GLAD TO HEAR YOU'RE DOING OK. 'CAUSE I'M

# ENGAGED . . .

LATER!

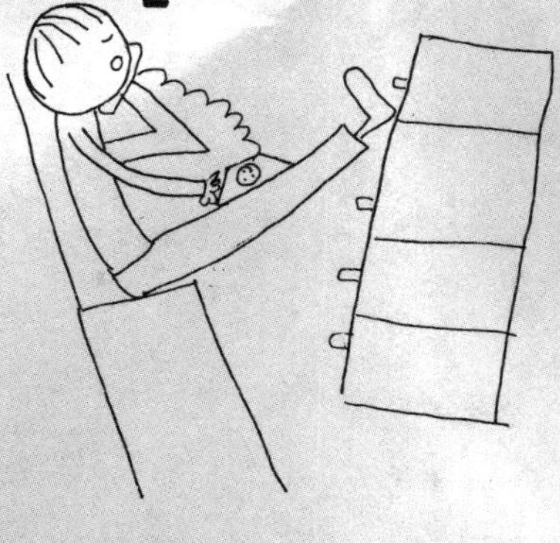

# Day 72

At this point if you are not really getting over it, you begin feeling kind of down in the dumps. I like to remind myself of how popular I am. And what fun I have with my friends. Buy a bunch of disposable cameras. Hand them out to your friends and go out drinking. And dancing. Then snap away. Admire how your life doesn't suck—it's really kind of fun, right?

<150>

<151>

Day 74:
Sign up for a wine-tasting class. No, this is not a cheesy way to meet single guys. It's a socially acceptable way to get drunk on a Monday night.

<154>

GROSS.

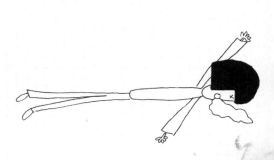

<155>

Listen to Carly Simon.
I like "Coming Around Again."
It's so very relevant. And
if a girl can get over a
breakup with James Taylor and
use it for inspiration . . .

<156>

. . . so it's a breakup calendar . . .

That's a dumb idea.

Become good friends with his ex-girlfriends. If he's really bad there should be a lot of them out there, so it'll be easy.

It's a small world

<158>

after all . . .

<159>

# Day 77:

Get on the Internet and look for people who can relate. Believe me, they are out there: The web is jam-packed with heartache. You're sure to find stories that are worse than yours. Nothing can make you feel better.

Well, actually, I can think of a few things, but they are way too violent.

<160>

<161

<162>

**Day 78**

Hiss at new couples.

<163>

# Day 79:

Burn old photographs
       of the two of you.

<164>

<165>

# Day 80:

Get rid of any odd items that you
may have lying around that could
possibly remind you of him.

<167>

## Day 81:

Write the name of your ex
10 times on a piece of paper.
Place a red candle on top of
the paper. When the candle
burns and lights the paper afire,

you will have hexed him.

<168>

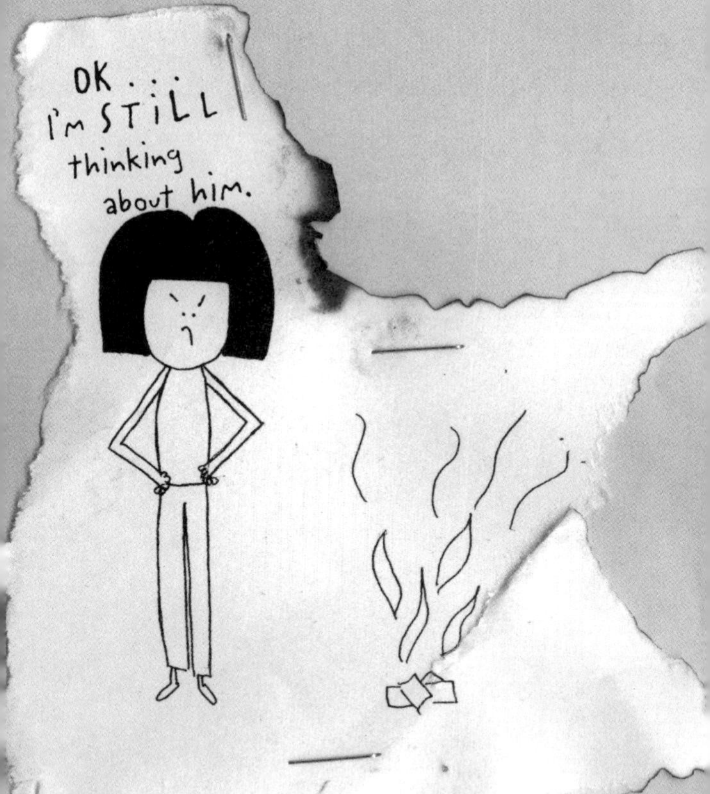
OK . . .
I'm STILL
thinking
about him.

# Day 82:

Make no mistake about it. You two are bitter enemies. You are Mia to his Woody.

<170>

Beware. EVERYONE you meet from
here on in will have the same
name as your ex. It's OK to hate
them.

<172>

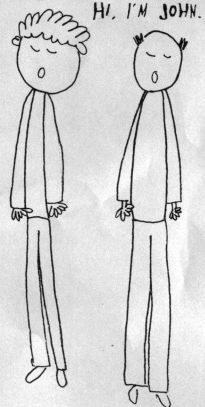

## Day 84

Amnesia would come in handy at a time like this. But according to my doctor it is very difficult, if not impossible, to self-inflict. Naturally, I want a second opinion, but in the meantime I've found that it is easy enough to develop a mental block.

<175>

# Day 85

St John's Wort.

- Ignore the instructions on the back of the bottle.

- Take as much as you like. Until you're full.

<176>

AMBULANCE

<177>

# Day 86:

Ignore any friends who have a
new romantic interest or who
have "all of a sudden" fallen
in love. All they'll want to
do is talk about how food
tastes better now, and the
sun shines brighter. It's
revolting, really.

<178>

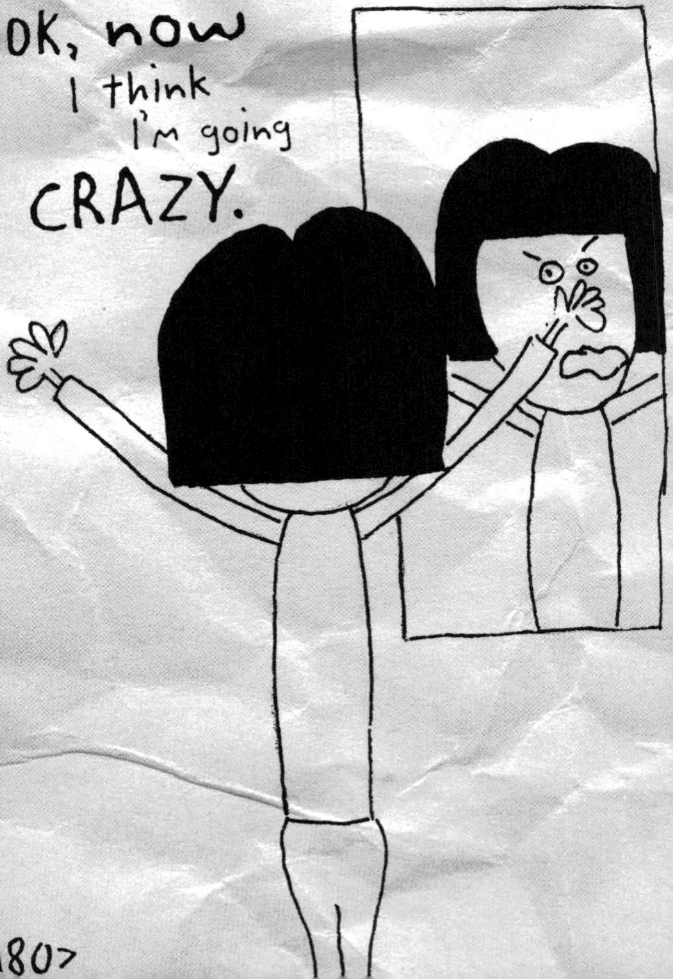
OK, now
I think
I'm going
CRAZY.

# Day 87:

Spend some time in front of the mirror practicing menacing looks. These will come in handy if you "accidentally" walk into his new girlfriend's office.

<181>

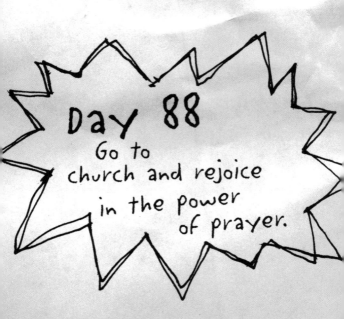

Day 88
Go to
church and rejoice
in the power
of prayer.

<182>

<183>

Day 89

Acquire a taste for hard liquor. And remember, if it's not brown, it's not worth it.

Do I LOOK like I care? Give me more liquor!

<185>

## Day 90:

Come to the realization that carbohydrates, not memories, are the real enemy. Develop an inexplicable taste for isolated protein solids.

<186>

<187>

Day 91:

Don't call him.

<188>

THIS

NUMBER

HAS BEEN

DISCONNECTED.

<189>

# Day 92:

Don't e-mail him.

:(

<191>

192>

# Day 93:

## DO NOT under ANY CIRCUMSTANCES get another cat. Otherwise you'll end up being that lady at the end of the block with 18 cats.

‹193›

# Day 94:

Don't feel guilty about
giving him a subscription to
<u>Playboy</u>. At work.

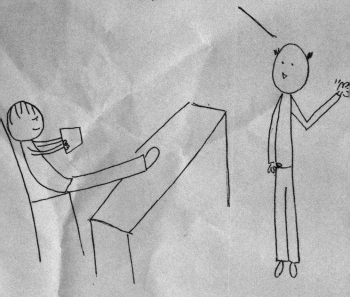

<196>

## Day 95:

Just tell everyone you know
that it didn't work out because
he turned out to be gay, and
you wish him well.

<197>

# Day 96:

Suddenly The Lifetime
Channel makes sense.

<198>

<199>

SUZI!
STOP CALLING US!
YOU BROKE UP WITH JOHN
3 MONTHS AGO
AND WE NEVER LIKED
YOU ANYWAY.

# Day 97:

Maintain your relation-
ship with his parents.

<201>

# Day 98

Make sure you have at least 3 good guy friends who will take you out and act as escorts.

<202>

<203>

# Day 99

Go to a party where he's bound to show up and have the time of your life.

 <204>

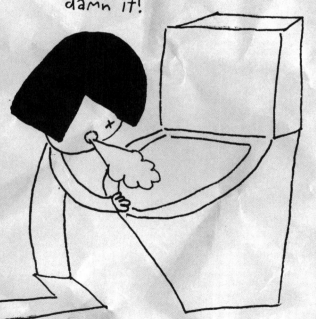

<205>

## ☑ Day 100

OK, so it's time to go over what we've learned.

- We are strong women who refuse to be kept emotionally hostage.

- We think with our heads not our hearts.

- And the next time we get into a relationship, we will gather fingernails, strands of hair, and flaked off skin for a voodoo doll. Just in case.

# Acknowledgments

Thank you Angelo, Ann, Anna, Asher, Cameron, Cara, Christopher, Clay, Frank, Isa, James, Kelly, Michael, Mike, Richard, Rotem, Scott, Sean, Tia, Tricia, Ucef, Whitney, and Dr. Marcuse.

## About the Author

Mandana Hoveyda is an award-winning copywriter and illustrator who lives in New York City. This is her first book.